© Shaun Willis

Mercy in the Fig Tree: Jesus Loves You invites you on a spiritual growth and renewal journey. Through heartfelt reflections and biblical insights, this book explores how God's grace turns brokenness into blessings, deepening your faith.

For more insights and resources, visit:

Shaun Willis
www.mercyinthefigtree.com
www.jesuslovesyou.art

Painting by
Scott phillips

TABLE OF CONTENT

Sand Washing away at the seashore	3
Our Foundation	7
His words and not ours	12
Every Grain of Sand	16
Every Word spoken,	19
Every brick laid	19
Idols & Idle Words	25
Sins	27
Holding back God's wrath	30
By Faith	32
Walking By Faith	35
Building Blocks	39
Reverent fear	41
Fears and doubts	43
Bearing good fruit	49
About the Author	52

1. SAND WASHING AWAY AT THE SEASHORE

During my 21 days of prayer and fasting in January of 2022, the Lord gave me a vision of sand washing away at the seashore. The only thing left, was a large grey cornerstone underneath the sand. The cornerstone represented Jesus. The sand represented my own words. I heard Him say that I had been building my house with my own words and not His words. This vision revealed how I had relied too much on my own words, much like the sand that can be easily washed away.

A week later, I was in my bedroom, and I felt the Lord's presence come over me, drawing me to my knees and leading me to pray to Him. In that moment, I did not know what He was about to reveal to me. What He revealed to me has forever changed my life, my pursuit, and my urgency to share the gospel.

Strap in and get ready for a ride. I was in complete and utter reverence and awe of how direct He was with me.

The Story of the Fig Tree

One day during my time with the Lord, I started reading the story of the fig tree. This story, found in the Gospel, spoke to me in a way that was deeply connected to what I had just experienced in my vision. You may or may not have heard this story before. He drew me to Luke chapter 13. I began to read about an owner and his gardener. The owner was becoming upset at the lack of fruit the fig tree was producing. The owner told the gardener that the fig tree was taking up space in his garden. He went on to say that he had come out to this tree for the last three years and had yet to see anything produced from it. He then told the gardener to cut it out and remove it from his garden. The gardener responded to the owner and said, "Give me one year, and I will give it special care and fertilize it. If it still does not produce good fruit, then I will cut it out and throw it away."

I immediately heard the Lord say that I was the fig tree. This message was meant as a warning that I needed to start producing good fruit. He went on to say that God had returned three years in a row and had yet to see good fruit produced. I immediately wept before the Lord.

A Plea for Mercy

The next morning, I cried out to God for mercy. I heard God say, "I have turned my eyes from you." And then I remembered that Jesus was the one showing me mercy, and so I turned to Him for mercy and grace. He embraced me and said, "I will speak to my Father on your behalf." I wept even more and felt a sense of relief and remorse that I hadn't been producing good fruit. I thanked Jesus over and over and over again. I laid belly down on the floor for a good while. By this time, I was crying with snot dripping from my nose. It was not a pretty sight to see. I was completely and utterly humbled before the Lord. I had nothing to offer but myself, which at the time didn't feel like much.

I sensed that my soul began to stir, the heaviness lifting as the Father's presence was drawing near. A part of me was being renewed, yet I knew this was just the beginning. In my heart, I was preparing for something deeper—a reunion with the Father, where I would finally turn and embrace Him once again.

A New Beginning

This is where the story begins. This is my prayer today for you as you read my story. Pray this as if it were your prayer:

"Lord, I need to receive your grace that you give when I let the sand in my life go. That sand representing my wrong beliefs, or simply my own words and not your words, and my own ways and not your ways. I repent right now from going my own way. Today, I choose to go your way! Amen."

If you prayed that prayer and meant it, it will change your life forever. Be prepared for additional actions and responses. The Lord will begin to call things out in your life. If you don't yet know what it is He wants you to give up, He will make it known throughout your day. Pay attention to your frustrations and problems throughout the day. Look for ways the Lord may be calling things out in your life that need to change and repent from. This is a new chapter and journey you have willingly chosen to go down. It will lead to many good fruits produced in your life from the moment you prayed that prayer, to the following moments that you will bend to God's will.

Today is a new day for you and me both. God is so good!!! Let's praise His name right now. Shout His name out. Give thanks to Him above all names!

I encourage you to take a moment to reflect on where you might be building on your own words instead of His. Consider asking God to show you any areas of your life that need realignment with His truth.

2.
OUR FOUNDATION

Wow, God is so good! If you are still here and reading on, I thank you for deciding to join me on my journey to becoming closer to Jesus.

> "Fear of the Lord is the foundation of all knowledge and wisdom." - Proverbs 9:10

This morning, I prayed for the Lord to guide our family and reveal to us what He wants us to do. I braced myself as I prepared for His answer, earnestly seeking Him. I was ready to respond to whatever His calling in my life was.

Then I wept and cried as I heard Him respond. This was the scripture He guided me to:

> "Looking at the man, Jesus felt genuine love for him. 'There is still one thing you haven't done,' he told him. 'Go and sell all your possessions and give the money to the poor, and you will have treasure in heaven. Then come, follow me.'" - Mark 10:21 NLT

I fell to my belly on the ground again and wept because I knew the Lord meant for me to sell the house, pay all my debts, and give to the poor. Then, our treasures would be in heaven. He said, "Then come, follow me."

I responded, "Lord, this command is too great and difficult for me to do alone. Give me strength to do your will. Send me your Grace to empower me."

It was too great because my heart was too full of worldly things that I worshipped more than I worshipped God. They became idols in my life. Idols can be very difficult to let go of because you love them. That's why you idolize them. Letting go of idols felt like stripping off a part of me that I didn't realize was attached so deeply.

The Lord reminded me of Proverbs 1:7, "Fear of the Lord is the foundation of true knowledge, but fools despise wisdom and discipline."

He taught me this morning that if I don't respond and obey Him, then I don't fear His words. He reminded me of the conversations we have with Collin, my son, about obedience and how when we do not act or respond, that is still disobedience.

I desire to be disciplined by Him.

I asked Him what following Him looks like. I asked Jesus to give me a vision for me and our family. After we sell the house and give it all to the poor... then what? Jesus says, "Come, follow me." I said, "Will you wait to reveal that vision after I have obeyed you?"

I told the Lord I will wait for His counsel, but in the meantime, He has spoken:

> "Yet how quickly they forgot what he had done! They wouldn't wait for his counsel!" - Psalms 106:13 NLT

I follow the Way:

> "I admit that I worship the God of our ancestors as a follower of the Way, which they call a sect. I believe everything that is in accordance with the Law and that is written in the Prophets." - Acts 24:14 NIV

I told the Lord I'm scared! I told Him, "What about my future retirement? What about my kids and their kids? How will I provide for them?!"

> "Trust in the Lord with all your heart and lean not on your own understanding; in all your ways submit to him, and he will make your paths straight." - Proverbs 3:5-6 NIV

I remembered that scripture, but do you remember the rest of that scripture? Continue to read down to around verse 26 or 29! Here is some of it:

> "Seek his will in all you do, and he will show you which path to take. Don't be impressed with your own wisdom. Instead, fear the Lord and turn away from evil. Then you will have healing for your body and strength for your bones. Honor the Lord with your wealth and with the best part of everything you produce. Then he will fill your barns with grain, and your vats will overflow with good wine. My child, don't reject the Lord's discipline, and don't be upset when he corrects you. For the Lord corrects those he loves, just as a father corrects a child in whom he delights. Joyful is the person who finds wisdom, the one who gains understanding. For wisdom is more profitable than silver, and her wages are better than free gold. Wisdom is more precious than rubies; nothing you desire can compare with her. She offers you long life in her right hand, and riches and honor in her left. She will guide you down delightful paths;

all her ways are satisfying. Wisdom is a tree of life to those who embrace her; happy are those who hold her tightly. By wisdom the Lord founded the earth; by understanding he created the heavens. By his knowledge the deep fountains of the earth burst forth, and the dew settles beneath the night sky. My child, don't lose sight of common sense and discernment. Hang on to them, for they will refresh your soul." - Proverbs 3:6-22 NLT

The Lord gave me a vision of us rebuilding our wealth on His foundation. He said to me that this act of obedience will be a sign and a remembrance of when we decided to not serve two masters—money and God—but laid money down to serve Him!

Great is your reward in heaven for fearing the Lord and obeying His commandments. He will use this to bless us and others around us more than we could ever imagine in this lifetime and in the next.

The Lord spoke to my wife from Deuteronomy chapter 6.

This is a text that I sent my wife:
"Honey, the Lord brought to my attention the Tesla Model Y and the idea of selling it, but I question whether it's from the Lord or not because we need a vehicle and this one will last a long time and is really good for our family. I want to do what the Lord is calling me to do, but I don't know if I am being blinded by my own desires and that is keeping me from fearing the Lord. I thought about selling it, but we still need a second car, so I asked the Lord could we sell the Mazda, close down Willis Wheels, LLC, and that be enough. I don't have any answers from the Lord this morning. I'm waiting patiently for His counsel. Maybe He is waiting to tell me when we sell the house? Pray for my heart to be

wholly committed to the Lord and any decision He calls us to make."

This was a snapshot—a peek into my wife and I's conversation. I knew going into this next season of life the Lord was asking for us to be wholeheartedly committed to Him by laying down every desire that is becoming an idol in our hearts.

> "By the grace God has given me, I laid a foundation as a wise builder, and someone else is building on it. But each one should build with care. For no one can lay any foundation other than the one already laid, which is Jesus Christ. If anyone builds on this foundation using gold, silver, costly stones, wood, hay, or straw, their work will be shown for what it is, because the Day will bring it to light. It will be revealed with fire, and the fire will test the quality of each person's work. If what has been built survives, the builder will receive a reward. If it is burned up, the builder will suffer loss but yet will be saved—even though only as one escaping through the flames." - 1 Corinthians 3:10-15 NIV

This verse confirms what I heard from the Lord—that in the next season of life, we cannot build our foundation using the wealth from the previous season. It has to be through the hard work of building our foundation on the Lord.

As we move forward, we do so with a renewed focus on His words and His ways, trusting that He will provide and guide us every step of the way. Our foundation is now firmly set in Jesus Christ, and with that, we embrace the journey ahead with faith and obedience.

3.
HIS WORDS AND NOT OURS

> "This is the meaning of the parable: The seed is the word of God." - Luke 8:11

I'm reminded of the Garden of Eden. The moment when the serpent talks Eve into eating the fruit. The serpent didn't bite, or try to strangle Eve to gain authority and dominion on earth. He simply was able to win her over by getting her to question God's words. And in this act, she submitted to the serpent and rejected God.

I took for granted the times Jesus spoke to me. I even questioned whether or not it was Him. I believe to a degree, asking God to reveal himself to confirm it was from Him, is good, but we must not doubt when we ask. Another way to discern if it's Him speaking, is if peace follows the voice. Peace doesn't equal comfort. A lot of times His presence walks us toward a direction that isn't comfortable, yet His peace remains.

Another way I discern God's voice is if my faith is stirred up. Faith comes from hearing the word of God. My pastor said once that when you're married you know your wife, but then after intimacy you KNOW your wife. He said that is the same with the Lord. That is why we are called His bride. An intimacy happens that brings us closer to God to discern His voice. My sheep will know my voice and they will come to me when I call. Since hearing my pastor share this, I was reminded of the moment that I felt my Heavenly Father turn His face from me and my desire to embrace Him grew even deeper. I knew that moment was coming when I would embrace Him and I would feel His presence and His love. It would be a moment I would never forget. A moment that would mark me for the rest of my life.

When I was baptized at 8 years old, Satan was angry. He didn't relent. He persisted to present to me things that would cause me to stumble through life. I spoke words of doubt, fear, and as though I was a guilty man walking. I was unprepared for the enemy's attacks. He strategized to deter me from getting to this point in my life. But the Lord has softened my heart from His consistent drawing me into His presence. I feel moldable like clay. I am a willing vessel for the Lord again.

I realize now the power of my words that I speak over myself, the thoughts that I allow to remain inside my head, and the words that I speak over others.

Pause here and ask yourself, 'What words have I laid in my foundation that might not align with God's truth?' Allow the Holy Spirit to guide you in uprooting any false beliefs.

I realize the power of God's word when spoken in faith. I realize when I speak His words over other's lives in faith, mighty things happen. God's word does not return void.

As I'm writing this I'm sitting on a bench and I see three paths that I could walk down. I'm reminded of the rest of that parable in Luke 8 "$_{12}$Those along the path are the ones who hear, and then the devil comes and takes away the word from their hearts, so that they may not believe and be saved."

On March 2023, the Lord brought back all my childhood memories before my eyes. He began showing me times where Jesus planted multiple seeds at 8 years old that led to me getting baptized. He showed me how the enemy tried hard to come in and take away the word from my heart. Then He realized that he couldn't destroy what was planted, so in his violent rage sent people into my life to try and redirect my path. He tried hard to place stumbling blocks in my life as distractions.

Like Eve in the garden, I was naive to the dangers of being independent of God because the fruit looked so tasty. After eating it though, it was bitter in my stomach. The guilt and the shame that followed and the hiding were all a part of the enemy's plan. His plan was to redirect my life away from a life of serving Jesus. The more I listened to the enemy, the louder he got in my life. I tried keeping secrets to appease my sin, so I wouldn't have to face it and deal with it, but that in turn made it even worse. A lot of tears were shed over the guilt and shame I felt. I got stuck in it and I didn't know how to get out. I didn't know that there was a way out. I grew up in Church, and I knew God loved me, but I never fully accepted it. I knew He forgave me every time I asked for forgiveness, but I felt powerless to make a lasting change and repent. I felt hopeless at times. I had spoke doubt after doubt after doubt over myself that I began to believe it. All the while reading God's word, but speaking doubt that I could ever change. I didn't know or understand my identity in Christ. I didn't know what it meant to be called His son. I never felt worthy.

In 2008, I started leading worship every Friday night at Celebrate Recovery at my Church. My dad called me one day and asked if I would be willing to step in and lead after their previous volunteer was moving out of state. I was moving back into town, so I accepted. It was here that I learned the power in confession. Confessing your sins to a group of men released guilt and shame which had a hold on me for a long time. Embracing the fact that I was a sinner in need of a Savior, was very difficult for me. It was humbling, but I still hadn't learned to openly speak faith and life into every situation. But It positioned my heart to begin to receive from the Lord. When I confessed, I admitted my need for a Savior. The enemy tried to do

everything he could to keep me hiding in my guilt and shame because in that place I was powerless and ineffective to the Kingdom of Heaven. In that hiding, the serpent has control over me, but the truth set me free.
In John 14:6 it says "Jesus answered, 'I am the way and the truth and the life. No one comes to the Father except through me.'"
In 2 Corinthians 12:9 it says "My grace is sufficient for you, for my power is made perfect in weakness." This is why I'm boasting in my weaknesses, so that His power is made perfect. And when God's power is present people are saved."
If you are reading this and you are not saved. If you don't know what it means to have a relationship with Jesus Christ, but you desire to... then say this prayer with now.
"Lord Jesus, for too long I've kept you out of my life. I know that I am a sinner and that I cannot save myself. No longer will I close the door when I hear you knocking. By faith, I gratefully receive your gift of salvation. I am ready to trust you with my life as my Lord and Savior. Thank you, Lord Jesus, for coming to the earth. I believe you are the Son of God who died on the cross for my sins. I believe you rose from the dead on the third day. Thank you for bearing my sins on the cross and giving me the gift of eternal life. I believe your words are true. Come, Lord Jesus, into my heart, and be my Savior and King. Amen."
Romans 10:9-10 says "if you declare with your mouth, 'Jesus is Lord,' and believe in your heart that God raised him from the dead, you will be saved. For it is with your heart that you believe and are justified, and it is with your mouth that you profess your faith and are saved."
If you prayed that prayer then rejoice! Please reach out to me, so we can celebrate together. If you do not have a church family then I would love to help you find one to call home. God intended for us to experience Him within the body of Christ, and to build one another up in Christ. The angels in heaven are rejoicing over your name today.

4.
EVERY GRAIN OF SAND

I see every grain of sand like every tear that has fell from my eyes in pursuit of Jesus. When I experience His presence, I find myself in awe and in reverence. I just melt in His presence as the lies, shame, and guilt flee from me. It is best summed up in Ephesians 5:26 "to make her holy and clean washed by the cleansing of God's word." I feel cleansed by the blood of the lamb. I feel redeemed in His presence. I feel alive.

Growing up I doubted God's word. My sins clouded my judgement. I would say one thing and do something completely different. James 1:8 "Such a person is double-minded and unstable in all they do." I was building my foundation on grains of sand. I was building on my own words and the words of others. When the storms come, they will wash away all that sand.

No storm came, but I felt His peace leave me. I felt anxiety, fear and worry set in. I wasn't prepared to deal with it. I now realize it was a slow release of His peace over a two year period.

When I repented, His peace came back. I realized if I am not moving toward God then I'm moving away from Him.

It is natural and easy to coast and build life with grains of sand. You become a victim to your circumstances. You react based on your situation, instead of responding with an outpouring of Jesus.

One thing I've noticed while building a foundation with sand, is that I had no idea there was a problem until the sea came from a wave to wash it away. Those moments are painful and humbling. Sometimes the waves are so calm that the pain of staying the same is not greater than the pain of having to change. This is similar to being lukewarm. In Revelation 3:16 "So, because you are lukewarm — neither hot nor cold — I am about to spit you out of my mouth." This tells me that I can't remain the same. I'm either getting worse or better. This all depends on our surrendering to Jesus as Lord. Romans 10:9 "If you declare with your mouth, 'Jesus is Lord,' and believe in your heart that God raised Him from the dead, you will be saved."

My declarations while I was a forklift operator were "I am a web developer". I believed that I was already a web developer and I started declaring it. I didn't see anything wrong with this declaration. I needed faith to achieve one of the greatest jumps in my career. Looking back, I started to see this declaration as faith in myself and in what I was accomplishing. I began to remove God from the equation more and more and my pride began to grow. It was creating cracks in my foundation. It was a grain of sand that led me down a path of buying things and taking on debt that I shouldn't have. It led me to lust after money and loving it. Buying Teslas, never happy with my salary because other software engineering friends were making more than me with the same amount of experience, and buying a house that had just been developed. These "things" that I was buying were not bad per say, but why I was buying them was not for a good reason. These things were beautiful to the eyes, but they came with a cost. I saw our extra income each month start to dwindle to where we no longer had the opportunity to help others. We were focused on just helping ourselves.

All it takes is one strong storm to come and wash away every lie and every word I told myself that didn't line up with The Word. I found myself also building on what others said in general or what they said about me. Putting someone's opinion of me over God's. It gives the illusion that your foundation is firm, when all your sand you have been building with is packed tightly together, until life comes with a wave too strong, washing it away.

On the Day, the weight will be on whether or not you believe in Jesus as Lord and to what degree. 1 Corinthians 3:13-14 "their work will be shown for what it is, because the Day will bring it to light. It will be revealed with fire, and the fire will test the quality of each person's work. If it is burned up, the builder will suffer loss but yet will be saved — even though only as one escaping through the flames.

5.
EVERY WORD SPOKEN, EVERY BRICK LAID

❝ Fear of the Lord is the foundation of true knowledge, but fools despise wisdom and discipline."
Proverbs 1:7 NLT

With one word you can tear down or build up. 2 John 1:9 "Anyone who runs ahead and does not continue in the teaching of Christ does not have God; Whoever continues in the teaching has both the Father and the Son." I find times in my life when I run ahead of God that I have to retract a word spoken. I have to walk through a period of restoration, either with people and God, or sometimes just with God.

Proverbs 1:7 "Fear of the Lord is the foundation of true knowledge, but fools despise wisdom and discipline."

John 7:38 "whoever believes in me, as scripture has said rivers of living water will flow from within them."

When we speak, rivers of living water should flow from within us. We are living in unprecedented times where we are connected to people we will more than likely never meet in person. We are more connected to every atrocity now from one click of a social media website or app. Anxiety and depression is at an all time high. How we speak to strangers and people we may never meet in person matters. We will be held accountable for every idol word we speak and for by our words we will be justified and by our words we will be condemned. Matthew 12:36-37 John 7:38 "Because he believes in me as the scripture says out of his belly shall flow rivers of living water." Our words come from deep within. When a person speaks is when we begin to discover who a person truly is. We are either programmed by our phones or programmed by the Word. Phones have become our biggest distraction, or it at least has for me personally. I don't want to speak for everyone, but in my own life it has. When I speak from that place, my words are harsh, impatient, quick to get angry, or annoyed. With our words, we can speak faith or feelings and doubts. With our words, we can speak life or death. If rivers of living water flow from our belly, then good fruit will be produced.

For every word spoken, I pray that it is from a brick that was previously laid, I'm finding myself going back to each scripture to remember what the Lord did.

Every "brick" represents scripture I lay in my "foundation" which represents my heart that needs to be firmly "planted" which represents my faith with "cement". "Cement" represents my actions which is made complete. In other words, every bible verse I put in my heart needs to be firmly planted by faith with every action I make. I am building with due diligence. I don't want to see one cracked brick in my foundation. So I go back to every bible verse that He has spoken to me and I remember the works that He did in me and through me. If I find that I laid a brick with haste and did not give thought to it then I uproot that brick for it will cause damage to my foundation. I filter out any of my words that are not lined up with His words.

I pray over every seed of faith, planting a hedge of protection over them.

God reminded me of Matthew 15:8-9 and it says their hearts were far from me. And in vein they worship me. I prayed Lord I confess that my heart has been far from you and I worshiped you in vein. Forgive me Lord. John 4:24 says God is Spirit and those who worship Him must worship in Spirit and Truth. I heard you Lord say wait patiently for me. When we speak let our voice be directed and motivated by the Holy Spirit.

"There is so much more I want to tell you, but you can't bear it now. When the Spirit of truth comes, he will guide you into all truth. He will not speak on his own but will tell you what he has heard. He will tell you about the future." John 16:12-13 NLT

I used to be a fork lift operator, but the Lord led me to change careers. I then became a software engineer. In the transition, though, I started building my foundation with my own words through self-affirmations. I would start to identify myself by saying I am a web developer and telling my wife that I am already a web developer, I just now need to get paid for it. This was great for building up my confidence, but I started relying on my own words. I started relying on my own self-assurance instead if what God's word says. During that time period when I began looking for my first web development job, the Lord lead me to volunteer at a weekend Christian retreat called "Chrysalis". It was during that weekend that the Lord led me to lay down my fears and worries of not finding a job and I decided to re-establish trust in the Lord as my provider. Jehovah Jireh. In Genesis 22:14 (KJV), It means "God provides." Genesis 22 tells a well-known story involving Abraham, his son, Isaac, and God. What I didn't realize at the time was the Lord was also wanting me to rebuild my faith and have it only in Him.

"Trust in the Lord with all your heart; do not depend on your own understanding."
Proverbs 3:5 NLT

In 1 Peter 2:4-12, it says once you had no identity as a people; Now you are God's people. My true identity is found in Christ Jesus. Everything I put my hand to prospers because it honors Jesus. I found my first development job the following week after I laid my fears at the cross. All my success has been because God my Father made a way for me. Like Moses after God defeated Pharaoh's army, He makes a way for me. He makes a way for those who love Him. Psalms 1:3 "He shall be like a tree planted by the rivers of water, that brings forth its fruit in its season, whose leaf also shall not wither; And whatever he does shall prosper." I am a Child of God. Say it with me, I. Am. A. Child. Of. God.

Here is all of 1 Peter 2:4-12, "You are coming to Christ, who is the living cornerstone of God's temple. He was rejected by people, but he was chosen by God for great honor. And you are living stones that God is building into his spiritual temple. What's more, you are his holy priests. Through the mediation of Jesus Christ, you offer spiritual sacrifices that please God. As the Scriptures say, "I am placing a cornerstone in Jerusalem, chosen for great honor, and anyone who trusts in him will never be disgraced." Yes, you who trust him recognize the honor God has given him. But for those who reject him, "The stone that the builders rejected has now become the cornerstone." And, "He is the stone that makes people stumble, the rock that makes them fall." They stumble because they do not obey God's word, and so they meet the fate that was planned for them. But you are not like that, for you are a chosen people. You are royal priests, a holy nation, God's very own possession. As a result, you can show others the goodness of God, for he called you out of the darkness into his wonderful light. "Once you had no identity as a people; now you are God's people. Once you received no mercy; now you have received God's mercy." Dear friends, I warn you as "temporary residents and foreigners" to keep away from worldly desires that wage war against your very souls. Be careful to live properly among your unbelieving neighbors. Then even if they accuse you of doing wrong, they will see your honorable behavior, and they will give honor to God when he judges the world."

During the month of January in 2022, I committed to 21 days of prayer and fasting corporately. At the end of that 21 days, the Lord revealed to me that every brick I was adding to my foundation were my own words and not His words. He told me that every brick I lay needs to be His words and if I find that they are my own words with no backing of His truths then I need to remove that brick from my foundation.

How many times have we heard a cool or encouraging saying and placed it in our foundation without questioning where it came from and if it is God's truth? Why would you build upon a saying that was outside of God's promises? Those words or sayings are not held accountable for what they tell you. They are empty promises made by the devil to distract you from the truth and to cause you harm. They can seem harmless at first but when you realize that brick was actually cracked, and you have already laid a ton of other bricks on top of it, now you have a foundation problem which can be very costly. It is better to find that damaged brick early and often then find it after you have already built upon it. So be intentional with what you start to believe and ensure the bible has your back. Be careful not to pick and choose scriptures in the bible that create a false narrative to make you feel good about what you are doing. Let the Holy Spirit guide you into all truth. But if you have already laid cracked bricks in your foundation like I did, remember there is hope. Jesus is our advocate with the Father, the righteous one! And He himself is the propitiation for our sins. 1 john 2:1

6.
IDOLS & IDLE WORDS

> " And I tell you this, you must give an account on judgment day for every idle word you speak."
> Matthew 12:36 NLT

"And he gives grace generously. As the Scriptures say, "God opposes the proud but gives grace to the humble." So humble yourselves before God. Resist the devil, and he will flee from you. Come close to God, and God will come close to you. Wash your hands, you sinners; purify your hearts, for your loyalty is divided between God and the world."
James 4:6-8 NLT

After having lunch with a good friend of mine, I left feeling something in my spirit was not right. There wasn't anything good or bad that we talked about in the conversation. Their was nothing really in it at all. I looked at the conversation as two guys shooting the breeze but not really getting anywhere in the conversation. At dinner, my spirit became even more unsettled. I didn't understand it. I felt my countenance had changed. I felt a disconnect from the Holy Spirit. The next morning, in my prayer time The Lord reminded me of a scripture I read the day before. It was James 4:6-8. I heard God my father say that your loyalty is divided. His presence overwhelmed me and lead me to repentance. I laid belly down on the floor and wept. I desire to yield my life to Jesus and when He shows up in the room, His power, authority, dominion and love walk into the room as well. If you haven't ever experienced the presence of Jesus and the Holy Spirit, then I would say this simple sinners prayer. "Father, I am a sinner not capable of saving myself and redeeming myself back into your presence. I believe and profess that Jesus is Lord over my life. I believe and declare that Jesus has saved me from my sins."

That happened on a Thursday morning, I shared my revelation and repentance from the idle words I spoke with friends the other day to Kim. Sunday, Kim told me that it lead her to repentance as well. She said that she prayed on the bathroom floor while the kids watched kids shows in our bedroom. She said "Lord, I'm not going to make any decision without you in it. She said the Lord started guiding her every step with peace. She asked God how they should do homeschool. She asked God how to speak to Collin. She said it was their best home school they have ever had." And the Lord gave Kim boundless amounts of energy.

1 Timothy 1:5-6, "Now the purpose of the commandment is love from a pure heart, from a good conscience, and from sincere faith, from which some, having strayed, have turned aside to idle talk"

This is my prayer for you today as you read this book.

Holy Spirit,
Put more reverence and honor into our hearts toward your words. Build up our faith in you so that we speak, act and move with you. Use us Lord for your will. Help guide us into properly honoring Your Name. The victory is found in the blood of the Lamb and our testimony. So let us profess our faith in Jesus Christ and be bold in sharing our testimony of the goodness of God. Amen.

7. SINS

Growing up in church, I learned the religious spirit very quickly without realizing what it was. I learned to hide sin and live as though I was sinless. As a kid in elementary who just committed their life to Jesus, I was learning quickly that there was a devil, a deceiver. I allowed him to feed me lies and give in to secret sins that allowed me to appear clean on the outside. The whole time I was condemning myself, Jesus was calling me home. He was loving me, and forgiving me. He was speaking life and hope into me, saying that I don't have to walk that path any longer.

During the same time I was baptized, Satan used people in my neighborhood and in my church even who were encouraging me to sin. We didn't have cell phones with access to the internet back then with such ease of access, but we had desktop computers that were able to access the internet. It tasted like a bitter yet sweet sin. I started lying to myself that it was ok because no one knew or was getting hurt by it. That was a lie of many lies that I convinced myself. Every sin you commit causes damage to you and others around you. Satan will do everything he can to prevent you from realizing that truth.

I look back all those years and I see how Jesus kept fighting for my life over and over again. Every Time I committed sin I saw a lash to his back that I caused. Jesus took every whip on his back that should have been my back. Every stone that should have been thrown at me, he held back through mercy and love for me.

Sin is a bondage that Satan deceives us into putting on ourselves. By doing this, he takes no responsibility for the sin or actions. The great deceiver who then uses the bondages to create a false identity in our lives. The longer we choose to live in sin, the longer his lies grow and begin to try and take root.

1 Peter 4:1 talks about how to be finished with sin. "So then since Christ suffered physical pain, you must arm yourselves with the same attitude he had, and be ready to suffer, too. For if you have suffered physically for Christ, you have finished with sin."

1 Peter 4:2, 6-8 says, "You won't spend the rest of your lives chasing your own desires, but you will be anxious to do the will of God. That is why the good news was preached to those who are now dead — so although they were destined to die like all people, they now live forever with God in the Spirit. The end of the world is coming soon. Therefore, be earnest and disciplined in your prayers. Most important of all, continue to show deep love for each other, for love covers a multitude of sins."

Even after years of bondage and being a slave to sin, God still had good thoughts toward me. Jeremiah 29:11 "thoughts of hope and a future. You may be feeling like I was when I was a slave to sin. The devil convinced me that I was hopeless, that I couldn't change, that it would always be this way. I spent nights in high school crying out to God for forgiveness. My double-mindedness prevented me from believing he could change me. In the midst of my hopelessness God was making a way. He is our banner of victory. He is our champion. He fights for me. He fights for you. Put your hope and trust in Jesus and lean not on your own understanding and He will make your paths straight. And in all your ways honor and glorify him. He frees the captives and he gives liberty to the oppressed. No sin is too great for the blood of Jesus. Let go of all the lies that you believed and believe in God's words. I was poor and he made me rich. I was bound up and he set me free. I was headed for the grave and he gave me life. All the sin, guilt, shame and bondage washed away through the blood of Jesus! By his stripes we are healed! But if you continue in sin you are of the devil. Repent. 1 John 3:8

8.
HOLDING BACK GOD'S WRATH

> "Since we have now been justified by His blood, how much more shall we be saved from God's wrath through Him!" - Romans 5:9

Kneeling down and praying I felt the warning from the Lord to produce good fruit. When I repented, I felt God hold back His wrath over me and my family. I wept with joy and relief. His words are life giving. When I'm weak, He makes me strong. When I'm tired and weary, He restores my soul and I fly high on eagles' wings.

Take this opportunity to reflect on God's power in your life. Are there areas where you need to surrender more fully to Him? Pray for His strength to fill those places of weakness.

Just when I start to tire, his Holy Spirit comes in and fills me up with boundless amounts of energy. I used to have doubts that it was indeed God moving in my life. I thought maybe its just my own emotions that are driving my beliefs and making me feel like something is happening and it's not. Let me tell you, that is far from the truth. I've since learned the power in your words when they align with God's words. Healing happens. Miracles happen. Harden hearts become soft!

If you have been far from God, take this time to repent. Ask for forgiveness and turn back to him. In doing so, you will have kept yourself from receiving the wrath of God.

9.
BY FAITH

Faith has been difficult for me most of my life, but not anymore. God began revealing to me through writing this book that it has been my sins entangling me that caused me to doubt God's word. My struggles led me to doubt, but now through God's word I'm choosing to trust in Jesus more and more. Hebrews 12:2 says "Looking unto Jesus, the author and finisher of our faith..." Like doubting Thomas, I fix my eyes on Jesus who began my faith. My doubts, my confusion and my struggles came from living with a liar. Listening to the enemy for so long I forgot there is someone who speaks truth and is trust worthy and faithful. His promises are as good as done. If you are struggling with your faith, fix your eyes on Jesus. Remember we are surrounded by a cloud of witnesses. Hebrews 12:1.

In Chapter 11 in the book of Hebrews, it talks about great people of God that showed great faith. I can't help but remember a couple of moments in my life where I one hundred percent could not have done what I did without faith in God. I think I can be too hard on myself and don't give God enough credit for the work he has done and is still doing in me.

The moments in my life where I believe I showed great faith have been... well.. let me just share some stories with you.

When I asked Kim's parents if I could marry their daughter, they ask me to commit to finding a solid job to provide for her. I was working for a friend of mine at his HVAC company but it wasn't stable. I told them that I would work at UPS to take care of her. Honestly, it is hard to believe that they said yes in that moment. I am so blessed with amazing in-laws who had faith in me. I released faith in that moment when I spoke with them. And about 6 months later in 2009, I was employed at UPS. I spoke in faith believing it would happen and the Lord guided my steps.

In 2016, while struggling to provide for Kim and our son, Collin, God started drawing me toward becoming a software engineer. I had faith in God that He would provide for my family and six months later, he came through. Because of God, I successfully transitioned careers and got out of the warehouse work for good by the grace of God. For six months, I had no income during the transition. I was all in. I had no plan b. I believe God rewards us when we have faith in him. And now God has blessed our family financially to where we don't worry about money anymore. We are able to give back to the community which was a prayer God has now answered. My brothers, sister and I were able to bless my dad with a brand new golf club set for his retirement. This is something that I would have not been able to do had I stayed in the warehouse. We have been able to give back to our local church. And lots more moments that I want to keep private between God, my family and myself. Because of my faith in God, Kim and I sold our brand new house. No one else had lived in it before us. It was gorgeous. We loved it, but we heard God call us away from materialism. Like Abraham, we left our home in faith. In the midst of that decision, Kim's parents had an idea that would mean we inherit their land and house early. Originally they were going to gift the house to Kim in their will when they passed away. When we began discussing what the Lord was doing in our life, plans began to form that included us inheriting their land and house now. God was moving in the midst of our conversations. If I had not been on this journey with God hearing directly from him that we should sell, I would have never been open to the idea of inheriting the property early.

With the sell of our house and the move onto her parent's land, the Lord wiped away every debt we had. I woke up on my 35th birthday debt free. It felt like the year of jubilee. I started writing this book in January of 2022 and by May of 2022 the Lord had blessed my family far beyond our imagination by paying off every single debt we ever had.

11.
WALKING BY FAITH

> "So you see, we are shown to be right with God by what we do, not by faith alone."
> James 2:24 NLT

It's September 2023, and my Pastor, Pastor Bill Adcock, revealed to me that the devil is like a roaring lion walking about seeking whom he can devour. 1 Peter 5:8.

In my mind, it was a harmless question with innocent intent.

In reality, it was manipulative in order for me to gain something I had personally been desiring. As I'm sitting in our prayer meeting, I hear the pastor say, "some questions you shouldn't even be asking." When we entertain ideas and suggestions that God isn't in, we get ourselves in trouble. To prevent from falling in to Satan's trap, we have to remain in the Word. You have to pray unceasingly.

Since the age of 8 years old, I have been walking with the Lord. That is almost 30 years. I still feel like my journey has just begun.

"So you see, we are shown to be right with God by what we do, not by faith alone." - James 2:24

James emphasizes movement... action. We can't just believe, we have to walk by faith and bring actions along with our faith. Then we are shown to be right with God.

1 John 2:3-6 "Now by this we know that we know him, if we keep his commandments. He who says, "I know him," and does not keep his commandments is a liar, and the truth is not in him. But whoever keeps his word, truly the love of God is perfected in him. He who says he abides in him ought himself also to walk just as he walked."

Let me be candid with you for a moment. Even though I was saved at 8 years old and I am now 35 years old while writing this in 2022, I have wrestled with the topic of healing for my entire life up until this point. Within the last two years, I have experienced and seen my kids and my wife healed. I began feeling a tug from the Holy Spirit to trust God more, be vulnerable and take a risk. I heard Him tell me to pray james 5:14 over my son one night when he became sick. I felt the peace of God rest on me and confirm that he would be healed. I began to walk in that confidence and trust Jesus more. While my son was sleeping, I put oil on his forehead, prayed james 5:14 over him and spoke in my heavenly language. The next morning, he woke up as though no sickness had came over him the night before. He walked straight into my room 100% healed of whatever bug that had overtaken him the night before. I used to be very skeptical of healings. I would argue it away in a logical sense and just say oh he would get better on his own from his body healing itself. I agree with that statement, but usually that takes days to get over. He got sick the same night I prayed over him and the next morning he woke up healed. I will be completely honest with you. Satan didn't want me sharing this story. I questioned it was from God many times because this was during a time when I began trusting and having faith in God towards healing. My mind was not fully rooted in His word at this time. I was shifting back and forth between whether or not I believed God healed my son. I now realize that it was the enemy trying to steal a victory. I realize now that when God moves in one's life, the enemy immediately comes in and attempts to steal, kill and destroy the seed that was planted. He does this by giving us questions of doubt. He did it successfully to Adam and Eve and he hasn't change his tactics since the Garden of Eden. If he can plant a seed of doubt that eats up the seed of faith, then he is able to subdue any future victories that would have came from the growth of that seed of faith.

I am here today to tell you that I believe with all my heart that my son was healed by Jesus Christ's stripes. The blood of the lamb healed my son. The Son of the living God. The Savior of the world. Whom I can call my friend. I had another instance of healing happen within my family. My wife just gave birth to our daughter. She was having pain in her hips. She asked me to pray. I laid hands on her fully believing God would heal her. When I finished praying, I told her to walk around expectant. She exclaimed, "it feels better!" She decided to take my son and daughter on a walk and while she was walking she began to doubt her healing. The enemy started planting seeds of doubt in her mind, but she recognized the enemy's tactics and she rebuked him. She reclaimed her victory in Christ. She continued walking out her faith and the pain from her hip subsided.

We have to fight for our faith in Jesus Christ, because our faith is constantly under attack from the devil. Our victories begin when we begin to stand on the Word of God and trust in the Lord while not leaning on our own understanding. The enemy will leave us alone if we read God's word but don't believe it and don't apply it. He actually has a field day with inactive and faithless Christians. The bible says to run away from believers who have a form of godliness but deny his power. 2 Timothy 3:5. These type of people are the most productive in promoting Satan's agenda and seeds of doubt. They steal future victories from believers who were discouraged from having faith in God. The most dangerous thing we can do as a believer of Jesus Christ is to start believing and obeying The Word. I fight for my faith and others now. I am encouraged and I look to be encouraging to others. I think of ways to love and encourage others in their faith journey abiding in the Holy Spirit. Jesus is the Author and Finisher of our faith. Hebrews 12:2. It's time we lay everything down, so we can walk by faith following Jesus from victory to victory.

12.
BUILDING BLOCKS

> "And because of his glory and excellence, he has given us great and precious promises. These are the promises that enable you to share his divine nature and escape the world's corruption caused by human desires. In view of all this, make every effort to respond to God's promises. Supplement your faith with a generous provision of moral excellence, and moral excellence with knowledge, and knowledge with self-control, and self-control with patient endurance, and patient endurance with godliness, and godliness with brotherly affection, and brotherly affection with love for everyone. The more you grow like this, the more productive and useful you will be in your knowledge of our Lord Jesus Christ. But those who fail to develop in this way are shortsighted or blind, forgetting that they have been cleansed from their old sins."
> **2 Peter 1:4-9 NLT**

It's been a year and nine months since I was first inspired to write this book. I'm finding myself hungering for his Word more everyday now. When I'm reading The Word, I find myself talking about his Word. My bible footnotes say faith is more precious than gold. I was reminded of the parable where the man finds hidden treasure in a plot of land. He sells everything he owns to buy the land, so that he can attain the hidden treasure.

I wrote this book originally to be a reminder for me and my family of what God has done in our lives. It was intended to be a way to encourage us when we lose heart. Our testimonies build our faith in God by reminding ourselves all the good God has done in our lives. It also encourages others to continue the race of faith until we attain our prize. By reading this book back to my family and myself, we build on the previous blocks of faith that God has cemented in our lives, which in turn, builds our confidence in Him.

13.
REVERENT FEAR

> "Fear of the Lord is the foundation of true knowledge, but fools despise wisdom and discipline."
> Proverbs 1:7 NLT

In Genesis chapter 3, Moses saw a burning bush not being consumed. When he turned to look at it's sight, God called out to Moses. God's first response was to direct Moses, "Do not draw near this place." God paused Moses because the position of his heart needed to be changed. Then God said "Take your sandals off your feet, for the place where you stand is holy ground."

As I am sitting down in a chair in a prayer meeting for men, I felt an urgency to take my shoes off after I read this scripture. Embarrassed, but obedient so I took my shoes off as discreet as I could. I felt the Holy Spirit rest on me. I imagined being Moses in that moment and what it felt like to hear God speak directly to me through a burning bush. I felt his love. This story may sound silly to some, and I laugh when I think about it, but I also am filled with joy. I feel so much joy because I know my heavenly father takes time to visit with me when I'm pursuing him. Every time I open up my heart to the Lord, he fills me with so much love and joy and energy to love others. I know God uses these small moments in my life, because I've seen him do it time and time again. Every time I position my heart to receive from Him he speaks to me. He builds up my faith in Him.

There is a book I'm reading called "Brainwashed" by Manny Arango that comes to mind. He said, "Conversely, the first foundational stone of the Mind of Christ is faith, belief, and trust. As we determine to make our first move from the Mind of Adam to the Mind of Christ, we must move from doubt and independence to trust and surrender."

A reverent fear of God leads me to trust and surrender to His will. He is the Way, the Truth and the Life. No one goes to the Father except through Jesus. John 14:6

14.
FEARS AND DOUBTS

❝ Doubts can creep in like a snake. It starts slowly through a word spoken that goes unfiltered or tested by the Word of God when we are walking around unaware of our enemy that is prowling about. Then unexpectedly, the enemy attacks when we least expect him too. He rears his ugly head, whether we are coasting through life or not. And how we respond to the enemy's attacks are a result of the accumulation of prayer, supplication to the Lord, and studying to understand the Lord's ways and his character. Or in my case, the lack there of. Doubt in the moment seems right to a man, because we deceive ourselves into thinking we have it under control. The enemy does a great job convincing us that we can be independent and make our own choices. He does a great job convincing us that we know better than God and that we are weak when we pray or call to God. In the end, this thinking leads to death. The enemy has used doubt as a strategy since the Garden of Eden. So this strategy is proven to work on Adam and Eve. This is why he continues to use it against God's children. I am reminded that we are not fighting against flesh-and-blood, but against evil rulers and authorities of the unseen world, against mighty powers in this dark world, and against evil spirits in the heavenly places. I'll say it again, I've never been more convinced than I am right now that God is real, He is who He says He is. I can trust in his Word. I will be dependent on every Word that comes from His mouth. He is the one who gives life and life abundantly. The enemy comes to steal, kill and destroy life. That is what we are up against every single day. The world has no hope against the enemy's tactics. They walk around blind and hopeless. They are consumed with rage and hatred. They are bound by their sins. They are a slave to their human nature and desires. But we as Christians have the hope of glory living inside us.

1 Peter 5:10
And the God of all grace, who called you to his eternal glory in Christ, after you have suffered a little while, will himself restore you and make you strong, firm and steadfast.

Whatever the thought or situation, the enemy looks for ways to plant seeds of fear, doubt, worry and anxiety into our hearts to steer us away. His strategies are intended to steal us from our victories, because Satan knows if he can do that then he can remove our reliance on God. He can make us hopeless for the future. He then makes us ineffective for the Kingdom of Heaven. We walk around knowing the Word of God, but convincing ourselves nothing will change. We walk around powerless. We become less effective on earth in planting seeds of faith in people's lives. We deceive ourselves by sharing scriptures with others, but not having any faith or expectation attached to that Word. Our purpose becomes entangled with our fears. We become driven by our fears instead of driven by the faith we have in Christ. We start to believe it is just God's will for us to be "this" way. When that is so far from the truth. And we know that the Holy Spirit is called the "Spirit of Truth". If we say we believe in God and confess Jesus as our Lord and Savior then we have an obligation to take Him at His Word.

And His Word says in Jeremiah 29:11 "For I know the thoughts that I think toward you, says the Lord, thoughts of peace and not of evil, to give you a future and a hope."

If we don't fight against the thoughts in our minds that attack God's character and make us doubt Him, then we are actively and willfully choosing to submit to Satan's authority. If we just accept every fear that enters our hearts, then we are full of contradictions to God's word. Our doubts and disobedience are the root issues causing us to stray away from the Lord. Then we live in this doubt and disobedience for so long we forget our identity in Christ. It is a dangerous and slippery slope. I know because I was headed in that direction. The bible says perfect love casts out fear. 1 john 4:18. We need to cast fear out continuously or we will become a slave to its demands. We will walk around powerless, while at the same time quoting scripture. We know the scripture, but it's not setting us free and we don't know why. It's because we allow every thought, idea, and doubt creep into our minds unchecked, unfiltered through the Word of God.

My daughter, Chloe, was showing a low grade fever and i felt consumed by fear when I told my wife, Kim, that I am finishing up at the office and I'm coming to pray over her. I laid hands on Chloe and prayed. But I let fear into my heart, so I knew my prayer wasn't as effective. I shifted and prayed a prayer of repentance for allowing fear to creep in. I prayed a prayer of rebuke against the enemy for attacking our family. I felt in my spirit that this attack was going to require me to dig in and not give up. The enemy caught me off guard and now I am fighting to regain ground that I once had.

God revealed something new to me in this situation. He doesn't just fight for me. He fights with me. This is because when I say to the devil "Get out by the authority of Jesus

Christ, and the blood of the lamb. I command you to leave" Jesus shows up in a mighty way. He destroys our enemies. Fighting back against the spirit of fear and the enemy brings freedom. It brings new revelations and new found faith. It brings joy and peace and liberation.

After I prayed over Chloe I couldn't eat my supper. Kim rightfully questioned me on why I wasn't eating and said that it was because of fear. I said if that is true then let me eat. Looking back now, I see that there are times we can choose not to eat because of stress and that doesn't please God. I was letting fear drive my decisions and the Lord cannot move through doubts. God can't work when we don't believe He can move. Our fear can be the very thing preventing us from a deeper relationship and reliance on our heavenly father. It is the very thing we need to move towards instead of running away and cowering.

If you look at the story of Moses, you will see where men disobeyed God when they had fear in their hearts. The One who had the power and authority to protect them, they decided to not trust. They decided to yield to their fears instead of yielding to God in faith. It sounds absurd, but it goes to show you how much power fear has when we submit to it. THAT is why we can't let fear creep in and remain in our hearts. It will take us down a dark path that we never intended to walk. It will drag us into a place that God never intended for us to live in.

Fear is an indication that your breakthrough is right around the corner if you will trust God can bring you through to victory. It requires us being willing to die to ourselves and at the same time have faith in the Lord's ability to bring us to a victory. God is our super power to overcome fear and the enemy. He is the "Hail Mary" play in football that always works. When we are down in the 4th quarter and 10 seconds left on the clock. He always shows up and shows out to make a spectacular play. A play for the history books. One that will continue to be remembered years after we are gone. God doesn't make promises like the world does and then turn around and break them. When God says that He is with us, He doesn't just fight for us, but He fights with us. He is in the trenches.

"but whoever listens to me will live in safety and be at ease, without fear of harm."
Proverbs 1:33 NIV

Jesus revealed to me the importance of fighting our battles along side God instead of Him just fighting it for us. I felt liberated after I fought WITH God. If I let God fight all my battles without me, then I miss out on blessings of freedom and liberation. God desires for us to walk as sons and daughters of the King of Kings. In order for us to do that, it requires us fighting and winning alongside God.

Chloe wasn't going to sleep for Kim since she wasn't feeling well, so I put her in our van and drove her around. As I am driving, I begin to fight against the fear that I felt with Chloe's low grade fever.

Previously while I was praying over Chloe, she kept saying no I don't like it. I felt by her saying that their was a spiritual attack going on. She normally folds her hands together and bows her head as we pray. This time she did not.

While I'm driving her in the car, I began to get a sense in my spirit that I need to say "Get out by Jesus' power and authority. Get out! You are not welcome here. I rebuke you in the name of Jesus, the blood of the Lamb and by all the authority given through Jesus to me. Get out," then I began to speak in my heavenly language. I felt in my spirit that it was leaving. It was a wild feeling. It felt like a weight the size of a volleyball leave my belly and through my chest and shoulders and then left me completely. I felt that God was with me and that He was fighting along side me. I was overcome with joy, freedom, and peace. I felt liberated from fears grip on me! Praise God!! Hallelujah!! Perfect love casts out fear - 1 john 4:18

When we let fear in, it changes us and that is why we have to fight against it in our lives. Otherwise, when we submit to fear and allow it to overtake us, then we are a slave to whatever it is that we fear in our life.

I didn't used to look at fear in my life as spiritual attacks from the enemy until recently. 2 Timothy 1:7 says "For God has not given us a spirit of fear, but of power and of love and of a sound mind". I begin to realize after deciding to believe what the bible says and also that perfect love CASTS out fear, I started to not accept the fear in my life. So I began to cast it out. That verse told me not to accept any fear in my life. There are more scriptures in the bible that tell us to not fear, so when we still walk in fear we are being disobedient to His Word. The men with Moses that feared the giants, sinned against God when they wouldn't go take what was rightfully theirs. They disobeyed God who told them the land is yours. Go and take it for I am with you. Here is a prayer that I've prayed that I would like to share with you and if you feel led, you can pray it out loud too.

Lord,
I pray that you continue to strengthen me so that I never let fear dictate or strip me of my obedience to you. Continue to plant seeds of faith that sprout up in my life and destroy any seeds of doubt that have been planted by the enemy. I speak to it right now, be cursed. Dry up and wither away. You have no place in my heart. You have no right to be here. I release faith over every situation in my life and in my family's life and the people I do life with. Amen.

15.
BEARING GOOD FRUIT

> "But don't just listen to God's word. You must do what it says. Otherwise, you are only fooling yourselves."
> James 1:22 NLT

Before a seed can bear good fruit, it must die and be buried into the ground. I woke up one morning at 3:49am troubled from a dream. So troubled I couldn't go back to sleep. While still laying in bed, the Lord put my mind at ease. But I couldn't help but meditate on the dream and God's word and what the dream could mean. I discovered some possible symbolism in the Bible, but nothing that gave me complete peace. It was a Tuesday morning and I typically have a morning prayer with men from church at 6am. I grabbed my coffee and went out the door like I normally would do. While driving, I continued to meditate on the dream and wonder if God was speaking in the manor I thought He was or not. In that moment, I was stopped at a red light waiting for it to turn green. I was so fixated on the dream that I didn't recognize that the light had turned green. As I went to drive forward, I heard a noise in the distance coming closer. My first thought was it was strange and sounded like a helicopter. Then as soon as I looked left, I saw a big black truck run the red light to cross the traffic. If I would have pushed on the gas when the light had turned green, I would have been T-boned. He was driving so fast and his truck was so big compared to my '05 Honda accord sedan, I'm confident it would have resulted in my death that morning. Life is so fragile, and we don't have any idea when our last day on earth will be. This book has been a message of urgency. To not delay in doing good and in sharing your testimony. I now look at that day as my last day on earth that I served my own desires above God's. I look at that being the last day that I chose to disobey His Word and doubt His promises. I look at it as the day that I died to my doubts about who God is and who He is to the people around me. I am now reminded of that day as the day I'm confidently standing on God's Word now and forever.

I want to end this book with two more testimonials before I close this chapter of my life and this book.

While leading worship at Impact Church in Murfreesboro, TN, I began to feel fear, doubt, and condemnation creep back in unfiltered. The enemy was speaking very loudly in my ear. He was trying to convince me that I shouldn't be up there on stage. He presented case after case before me from all the times that I failed. I almost let him disqualify me, but my faith was building from hearing the Word of God. I began to confess the Word of God over myself all while leading worship. As I was hearing the enemy condemn me in my ear, God started breaking the hold that the enemy was having over me. I rebuked the devil and he fled. God gave me this image of satan transforming into a small fly. Then I swatted him away. At that moment, I felt from my head down to my toes a flash of lightening surge through my body. Instantly, the enemy's power over me shrunk and I no longer felt his hold over me.

Lastly, I want to share a story that may sound simple to some, but to me has felt as though it has touched the very depths of my soul. It was day 17 of 21 days of prayer in the month of August 2024. I prayed a dangerous prayer. In my spirit, my faith in God was now feeling more real then the air I breathed. I knew as soon as I spoke to God, I had no doubt in my mind that he was about to show up. Before I even spoke a word to him, I knew He was on his way to me. I had great expectation for this visitation with my heavenly father. For 16 days, I prayed for this one moment with the Lord. And on the 17th day, he answered my prayer. The prayer went like this... "Daddy, I know you are real. I know you are more real then the air I breathe. I know you are more real than these clothes that I'm wearing. More real then the food I eat and enjoy everyday. I have seen how you have showed up in my life time and time again. Even through my doubts, you were there working hard to reach me. Thank you, daddy!" Then the Father gave me this vision of Him walking through the veil. I remember asking myself if this is real what should I do? How should I respond? I did the only thing that felt natural. I ran to Him and hugged him. And the entire weight of the world was lifted off me, because I had my daddy in the room with me. I now know everything is going to be ok.

When Pastor Bill told me about this moment where you go from just knowing God to actually really KNOWING God because of the intimacy you experience with Him, I yearned for it. I had no idea what it would feel like or be like. I previously had moments with the Lord that were beautiful, but they were nothing like this. They felt similar to when you are dating your spouse. I can say with confidence now that God is forever now, my daddy. And I am His son. No one can convince me otherwise. I KNOW Him now. And I know He loves me as His son.

John 10:27-30 "My sheep hear My voice, and I know them, and they follow Me. And I give them eternal life, and they shall never perish; neither shall anyone snatch them out of My hand. My Father, who has given them to Me, is greater than all; and no one is able to snatch them out of My Father's hand. I and My Father are one."

ABOUT THE AUTHOR

Shaun Willis grew up in the heart of Tennessee, where he was born and raised. His deep-rooted love for his home state is matched only by his love for his family and his faith. Shaun is married to his beautiful wife, Kim, and together they have two wonderful children, Collin and Chloe. His family is his greatest inspiration and the driving force behind everything he does.

Shaun's spiritual journey began early in his life. At the tender age of eight, he was baptized in an old church in Manchester, TN, a place marked by its distinctive big church bell. This significant moment laid the foundation for his lifelong commitment to his faith.

Active in his local church, Shaun volunteers as a worship leader, sharing his passion for music by singing and playing various instruments. His dedication to worship and service extends beyond his personal calling; it is a shared journey with his wife, Kim. The two met in high school, and their love story blossomed within the walls of their church. As high school sweethearts, they have been inseparable ever since, united by their love for each other and their faith.

Shaun and Kim have been actively involved in two church plants. Through these experiences, they have witnessed firsthand the challenges and rewards of shepherding the Lord's flock. Although both church plants eventually closed their doors, the valuable life lessons and spiritual growth from those times have left a lasting impact on each of them.

Today, Shaun holds a deep sense of gratitude for the leadership at the church he volunteers. The support and guidance he receives continues to nurture his spiritual growth and fuel his desire to share the gospel.

"Mercy in the Fig Tree: Jesus Loves You" is a testament to Shaun's faith journey, his commitment to living a life that bears good fruit, and his passion for spreading the message of God's love and mercy. His story is a reflection of his personal experiences, spiritual revelations, and the unwavering belief in the transformative power of faith in our heavenly Father.

www.ingramcontent.com/pod-product-compliance
Lightning Source LLC
LaVergne TN
LVHW012249070526
838201LV00092B/169

i